Lose Weight Now!

These tips really work!

Sarah D

ISBN 978-93-5610-963-6
© Sarah D 2022
Published in India 2022 by Pencil

A brand of
One Point Six Technologies Pvt. Ltd.
123, Building J2, Shram Seva Premises,
Wadala Truck Terminal, Wadala (E)
Mumbai 400037, Maharashtra, INDIA
E connect@thepencilapp.com
W www.thepencilapp.com

Author biography

This book is about a girl who never gave up.

That girl could be you!

She had her hard moments when people said she was too fat to fit into a nice dress she felt she could wear.

She had those moments when people said she looked funny while exercising but did it anyway.

She had those moments when it was hard to avoid what everyone around her was eating.

She had those moments when motivation was the only problem inspite of knowing all of the health risks.

Sarah D is a person who is not perfect but did try to be it.

"No harm in trying so they say. Sometimes trying might get you somewhere"

Quotes like this can often be found in popular social media. She then decided to lose the extra weight. She is not the skinniest person you will ever meet, but she did manage to lose a startling amount of weight and she believes that her advice can help you get somewhere in your weight loss journey!

Like other women her age she has troubles maintaining a healthy weight and exercising. She believes that the right kind of effort can indeed get you somewhere!

CONTENTS

When there is a will, there is a way!

Why Healthy Eating Might Be The Most Practical Way To Lose Weight!

Eating Healthy is the single most important contributor to weight-loss!

Start off your weight-loss journey right! Get a hold of your eating habits!

You will start to see results! Eating Healthy is a really smart thing!

'A healthy outside starts from the inside' -Robert Urich

Eating healthy is a really great thing! There are many people who think they can eat as many burgers as they want, and they will still lose weight! There is nothing more 'wrong' than the above statement! So also the idea of comfort eating! People tend to indulge in unhealthy snacking whenever their mood tells them to do so.

I remember someone I knew who reached for potato chips, chocolate chip cookies, ice cream and anything else that happened to be in the house whenever she was feeling emotional about something. When she was stressed she reached for the chips. When she was happy she reached for the chocolate chip cookies. and when she wanted to relax in front of the tv she reached for the ice cream.

So maybe you cannot avoid snacking, but you can do something else that is phenomenal. You can choose to eat healthy!

What healthy eating is all about? Healthy eating includes avoiding foods that make you put on weight. You might have heard it all before. Remember that, none of this is bad advice. It's just hard advice!

 Basically, healthy eating can also refer to the avoidance of processed foods! Though the resolve to 'healthy eating' varies from person to person, losing weight usually means clean eating to some extent or the other!

So as a result of your healthy eating intiative, you are avoiding processed foods, and eating more fruits and vegetables! That is a very good thing! Even if you think you are not yet seeing any positive out come, you are getting fitter from the inside out!

Now I'm not saying that eating less bread or rice is the way to go! These things are indeed helpful, but if you have only just started out on your weight-loss journey, these tips are likely to be a little harsh on you. Rigid dieting will cause you to have setbacks like uncontrollable cravings followed by bouts of binge-eating, just to replenish the lack of energy.

Sometimes losing weight is about not comfort eating! Maybe every time you experience an event that makes you sad, you reach for the box of cookies in your fridge! Better believe it, at this point, replacing the high calorie option with its healthier version, is likely to have a variety of benefits. Some healthy food swaps one can make include:

- Having Greek Yogurt instead of mayonnaise.

- Try to replace cheese, butter and other spreads with nut butters like peanut butter and/or Avocado.

- Replace the sugar you add to your teas, and coffees with honey or artificial sweeteners

- Try a low fat ice cream instead of the regular full cream milk ice creams

- Swap the huge milk cadbury for a bar of dark chocolate

- Try soya chips instead of regular potato chips

- Try to replace deserts and pastries with the eggless variety

- Replace red meats with white meats like chicken or fish

Some of the benefits of making healthy swaps include:

- Ultimately, you will experience weight loss

- feeling fuller (without loading up on toxins)

- Feeling less hungry and feeling satiated throughout the day

- getting better nutrition in the form of things your body really needs like proteins, carbs, healthy fats and fibre

- overall better health

A lot of people choose to make these swaps, and they are so much healthier because of it!

What comfort eating is !

Remember that healthy eating is different from comfort eating in that sense only! Someone who over-eats is defying the laws of nature. Eating even after your stomach is full will lead to Obesity! You are eating more than your body is capable of digesting! It then becomes a habit! Science has proven it, the more you eat, the bigger you get!

If you happen to be a comfort eater, you are one of those people who are accustomed to rewarding yourself with food! Every time you do something good you overeat! Every time you achieve a goal or do something praise-worthy, you want to reward yourself with food! You go to the store and buy a whole tub of ice cream!

Many more people than I realize do this! It can be very comforting to over-eat sometimes. That's actually the reason for the bulge you notice in the mirror over the next few weeks and months!

A few things you should know about Healthy Eating:

May help you live longer

Making a decision to eat healthy is a concious choice that can help tonnes in the future. I suppose we all feel more than wonderful when we look at our reflection in the mirror and like what we see. Apparently the benefits of healthy eating are too many to outweigh. Literally. Consider that, taking the effort to avoid an unhealthy meal and cook it yourself at home could mean the difference between life or death. Consider that people who have less obesity related illnesses tend to live longer.

Boosts Immunity

Since the average "healthy individual" whose weight can be regarded as normal for his height is seemingly healthy from the inside out, his immunity probably is pretty good too. He or she might also have boosted their immunity by putting less strain on the body in the form of other health problems. Lets not forget that healthy food that mostly includes fruit and veggies in large proportions supplies the body with vitamins and minerals which also boost immunity.

Strengthens Bones

A sound mind and a sound body in a healthy body so they say, but did anyone ever think about healthy bones. Eating the right kind of foods is extremely good for the bones, including the fact that losing a bit of weight takes pressure off your knees!

Improves Digestion

Hyper palatable foods are not considered the best for the digestive system, as they do not have enough fibre. Why do we need to have foods that have fibre in them. Simply because fibre helps to store water which helps with the digestion process and passage of the dreaded toxic stuff out of the body. Fibre in fruit and vegetarian food also acts as a scrub brush to further cleanse the intestinal tract and be a harbinger of good gut health.

Slows down the aging process

You guessed right! People who eat healthy look younger because they have been supplying everything their body needs for wear and tear and ofcourse, repair. Can you blame the fact that a sweet n young looking person supposedly has less cellulite which ofcourse is nothing but less excess fat under the layer of skin known as the epidermis.

Reduces risk of lifestyle-related diseases

Finally healthy eating is the absolute preventative way to reduce the risk of coronary heart disease and diabetes and other lifestyle related diseases. Eating fruit and veggies can do that..go figure, I want more of those

Healthy eating has a number of benefits! Given above are just a few of the benefits of healthy eating. Making healthy food choices often leads to a healthier weight! Sometimes when you make healthy food choices, it reflects in your lifestyle. You find yourself making even healthier choices every day!

They say that one thing leads to another, when we start making healthy choices! Eating healthy affects us in good ways! The very fact that we are putting in the effort means something! Usually, wonderful things happen when you start doing something important like taking care of your health! One good thing leads to another! Hard work almost always pays off!

What does a healthy diet include?

A traditionally healthy diet includes all those things that are considered good for our health! A really good synonym for a healthy diet is a "Balanced Diet"! But what includes or makes up a 'Balanced diet'?

A balanced idea of nutrition supplies all the nutrients the body requires with things like "Proteins, Carbs and Healthy Fats"! Some healthy sources of protein are Chicken, Salmon, Eggs, Peanut Butter etc. Healthy sources of carbs include Milk, Bread, Pasta, Legumes etc. Healthy sources of fats include Avocados, Cheese, Dark Chocolate, and Whole Eggs.

Even if you never heard of the terms like "Proteins,Carbs and Healthy Fats", truth be told, people who take the trouble to educate themselves on what these things are, will be much fitter than those who don't. So, make sure that you feed your mind with health-friendly topics. Perhaps changing the channel when the Junk Food ads are on really is a good idea.

Coming back to the topic of trying to eat a balanced diet, make sure that you eat more of vegetables and fruits, drink enough milk, and eat lean meats like fish and chicken. Remember also that cooking what you eat, is a better idea, because you get to choose how much of each ingredient you put into your own food specially when it comes to things like oil, butter, cheese, margarine etc. The problem with dining out is that at restaurants, indiscriminate amounts of oil, butter, mayonnaise, ghee etc are used. While this might definitely up the taste factor, it does not do any justice to your waistline or your cholesterol levels either!

How to stick to a healthy diet?

Healthy eating is about more than just following some strict rules that are so hard to implement! It is about being mindful of the choices we are making on a daily basis. Making small changes like replacing a craving for a pizza with a bowl of fruit salad, or drinking a glass of water instead of a candy bar is part of it!

It's never easy making "healthy food choices"! We ought to try every day to resist processed foods that we are so tempted to enjoy by the vast variety of ads and billboards! It's always hard to say no to the coke and have a glass of water instead! I suppose that we now understand why they say "Doing what is worth it is never easy! Easy is what everyone is doing!

A few good ideas that can help you stick to healthy eating habits!

It's never easy to eat healthily! However, there are a couple of things that can help us to stick to our healthy eating habits!

Maintaining a "healthy eating" journal helps so much

Using a journal to track your eating habits is so worth the effort. By doing so you force yourself to acknowledge and remind yourself about what you are feeding yourself. It is usually considered an extremely good idea to maintain a food journal to record your healthy eating habit and motivate yourself.

Forgiving oneself, when they make mistakes

You may have had a minor slip up when it comes to making a healthy choice when it comes to every meal. However remember that choosing the unhealthy option once in a while is forgivable because we are human after all. It can happen that something irritating happened and you wanted to treat yourself with food. However, eating unhealthy once in a while is forgivable. We are all a work in progress.

Trying to use more health apps on one's phone.

Using health apps on your phone are another great way to keep track of what you eat, as they reccommend the average amount of calories you ought to eat in a day, just so there is nothing extra that needs to burn off. These apps really work because some of them even have coaching and exercise plans that are suited to you.

Getting a support circle either online or in real-life

Find a buddy who is going through the same struggles as you are everyday. Someone who like you wants to rebel, and wants to be a better version of themselves. A supportive friend who is also fighting the weight loss battle might help to keep the weight loss resolutions even when it is hard to do so.

Setting realistic weight loss goals
Having a realistic weight loss goal makes it all the more easier to reach. If you say you want to lose 10 pounds, you know thats next to impossible. But if you consistently lose 1 pound every couple of months acheiving your goal might actually be a goal that you can reach.

Setting smart goals that are practical and reasonable is a great way to finally make the number on the scale decrease. Some practical goals **you**can set are:

- I will walk energetically for 30 minutes at least 3 days a week

- I will avoid all soft drinks and snacks

- I will reward myself with a treat for eg getting a manicure, or getting my hair done on my cheat days

- I will watch encouraging things on social media that encourage me and help me to strengthen my resolve

- I will try and include more fruits and veggies in my diet

- I will try and make healthy food swaps and do meal prep

How long does it take to see results?

There ought to be a deficit between the amount of calories you consume, and the amount of calories you actually consume on a daily basis. You can expect to see results pretty soon if you burn more calories than you actually consume.

Better believe it, all of the above tips can help pave the way to a fitter you! Choosing healthy foods today will help you tons tomorrow! You might wonder if the number on the scale is ever going to budge. You have to be patient if it doesn't at first!

Sometimes health isn't about weight loss! Sometimes healthy habits when ingrained and learned slowly and made part of one's lifestyle can have more healthful effects and these effects are also longer lasting than a woman who loses 20 pounds or more just to fit into a dress.

Losing weight to look good in clothes is not a bad thing! But you can still enjoy your body in its natural state. Don't wait to achieve your fitness goals to make the best of who you are. Having realistic expectations is part of the deal!

Fun fact

Did you know that diet culture revolves around eating calorie-dense foods! Don't believe me? Go to a party and try eating a salad only, in front of whoever you are with- your boyfriend, your BFFs, your colleagues, anyone. You are sure to feel uncomfortable!

Unless it's something you have made a routine of doing! Unless you have a ready-made answer for when your pals ask you 'Why are you only eating salad?'

So here I thought I'd teach you, my readers, a new word. This term is called "hyper-palatable" food. Hyper palatable foods include all the processed foodstuffs that people carelessly tend to eat on a regular basis. Supposedly tasty foods like burgers, chips, pizza, and tortilla rolls.

As easy as it may sound, choosing healthy foods over unhealthy choices is never as easy as it appears. One really has to commit to a lifestyle change. And you guessed right, that often involves choosing to stay home, instead of hanging out with friends. This is because often hanging out with your buddies means eating the way they do!

Remember that choosing to eat healthily while avoiding high-calorie snacks, is considered a very good idea. Remember that its too much of a good thing, this choice you are making. There is a good old quote that goes something like

'If you don't treat food as your medicine, medicine will be your food.'

A few practical tips to help you avoid eating more processed foods:

- Whenever you go shopping, refer to a pre-prepared list and dont shop on a whim

- Do basic meal prep ahead of time, this helps avoid snacking on something out of the ordinary

- Try to avoid eating at restaurants, since restaurants famously use unhealthy igredients in food

- Cook more at home, because you, yourself, get to choose the ingredients, lol

Feed your mind positive messages, watch videos that exonerate your healthy food habits and make you feel good about them. Close your eyes when the junk food ads are going on. Look elsewhere! Believe me, this tip works!

- Join a support group for people who are committed to eating healthy. This way you will not feel alone!

- Enjoy your cheat days

- Reward your efforts with non-food rewards

Following a 12 hour fast

Usually following a 12-hour fast is considered ideal. There is no need to push one's self too much and diet too much. Also called intermittent fasting, a person eats during a 12-hour window, and fasts for the remaining 12. During the fasting period, he is to abstain from everything unless he decides to have water. Usually eating dinner at an early time makes this possible. Having dinner at 8 pm would require that the person eats their breakfast at 8 am the next morning.

This type of fasting helps keep the Circadian rhythm going. It ensures that proper digestion takes place, and also along with that the body's healing and repair processes.

Drinking Enough Water is the thing to do!

It is indeed considered very, very important to drink water on a daily basis!

Drinking enough water is a must, and ought to be part of routine!

Aim to drink between 8-12 glasses of water every single day!

Drinking water is essential to a healthy lifestyle-Stephen Curry

Drinking water is very effective in the case of weight loss!

That's a really smart thing to do! Why do I think it's smart? Research has shown that the more water one drinks, the easier it is to lose weight!
It is a good idea to try and cut back on sugary drinks, and aerated beverages- It could help if you drank less alcohol! Water is a zero-calorie drink, so drinking more water is a really, really good idea!

Some of the best reasons why water can be a great weight-loss aid :

- Water makes you feel fuller.

- Water has 0 calories.

- Water helps flush out toxins!

- Water is really great for your skin.

- People who drink more water are healthier and fitter overall.

- Water is completely natural and contains no added chemicals.

Water is such a great replacement for the other things that people tend to drink! I personally know a lot of women who cannot stomach a lot of water because to them it is 'tasteless' and they would rather have flavoured water!

It is recommendable to add more H2O to your diet because of obvious reasons! Water is really good for your health! I was using a diet tracker app (that I won't name) from Google Play. When I signed up for the premium version I was assigned a diet coach named Aditi, who really was the best!

What a fitness expert told me

They say, it's not the coach that brings out the best in us, but our own enthusiasm and willingness. Aditi kept track of my diet activity, calling me every weekend to check my weight. Aditi also checked on whether I was recording my progress daily in the app.

Aditi told me to Drink '8 to 12' glasses of water every day! I really feel this was the best advice she gave me! Every time I feel a craving, I have some water instead! I really do think I'm eating a lot lesser in general than I used to just because I drink more water!

Did you know that water is a natural appetite suppressant?

There are a number of reasons why. The more water one consumes, the healthier one is, literally. The body is 70% water anyways. Water helps to naturally suppress appetite because

- Water makes you feel full

- Water helps to avoid dehydration

- Water flushes out toxins

- Water helps to burn fat

Some of *the best reasons* to drink water are the ones given above- Sometimes though it helps to know the science behind the magic. You might be wondering how and why does water make anyone feel full? Water takes up place in the stomach, and thus it reduces the need to eat more. On the other hand, a need to eat often needs to be replaced by the need to drink for really good reasons. We might experience a craving, but we can consume less if we drink a glass of water.

It is obvious that water lost from the body through sweat etc. can be replaced by drinking more water. In that sense, Dehydration can be avoided. But how does water help to flush out toxins? When the kidneys have enough water in them, you can prevent constipation and everything flows out well. Water helps to metabolize fat and helps with exercise too!

Science tells us that life on earth would not be possible without water. Can you imagine putting yourself through that same condition of dehydration? Drinking enough water is a must, and when you drink enough water, you enable the body to do its regular function. Water is more than just a weight loss aid, you know! Water is part of the body, and a body that isn't hydrated isn't considered healthy!

Some other not-so-obvious benefits of drinking water:

- Perhaps you were unaware, but water boosts skin health

- Water lubricates the joints

- It also does a wonderful job of regulating body temperature

- Water flushes out toxins

Remember to drink enough water! Drinking adequate amounts of water is considered as an indispensable part of any weight loss program! The more water you drink, the better!

The Benefits Of Exercise are too many to count!

Sometimes watching what you eat, isn't enough! You may need some exercise as well!

The benefits of exercise are endless! Exercise is just another fancy word for increased physical activity!

Exercise helps to burn off calories by creating a deficit between the amount of calories you have consumed

and the amount of calories burned. Exercise also strengthens the body, since we develop the muscles

every time we perform any vigorous physical activity.

Exercise not only changes your body, it changes your mind, your attitude and your mood! - unknown

Exercise is good for everyone

Better believe it! You may think, "I'm too fat to exercise"! Exercise is so effective in aiding weight loss! People who exercise are more likely to lose weight than those who don't!

Exercise burns calories. It is scientifically proven that people who exercise lose a lot more weight than people who just cut back on what they eat. Many notice that they are starting to lose weight after eating less but then they reach a 'plateau'. A Plateau is when a person has been losing weight consistently for a little while but they cannot lose more weight than that. You may not believe me at first but breaking through plateaus of this sort, requires not only eating lesser calories a day but burning these calories as well!

Exercise is good in moderation

Exercise is good for you when you do it in moderation- I'm not a fan of the whole 'Fat is just sweat crying ideology'! Whenever I look on the internet for good weight loss motivation, I notice the use of words like 'sore', 'thigh gap', and 'do it for the collar bones'! Though these things are achievable, they are not possible for everyone!

I know a lot of people who get into an exercise regimen and only give up later. Sometimes words like moderation are so much better when it comes to YOUR exercise regimen because that way you will actually pull through every workout, be dedicated to doing every workout, and actually come back to workout without being 'too fatigued or in pain'

Many beautiful, attractive women I know exercise 3 times a week for 30 minutes. They are the best looking than they have ever been, and they are healthier because of their exercise habit!

Try and get a support partner to exercise with

If there is someone supportive around you when you are exercising, you are likely to exercise more effectively because of their support. Remember that having a buddy around you to exercise with is not only motivating, it's also freeing. Exercise in groups is more fun! Trying to exercise with a partner is one of the smartest things you can do to improve the quality of your workout experience! You are likely to train harder when you have someone who you feel supported by to work out with you!

Exercise that works?

I don't recommend over-exerting one's self, but even the little that one does help in the long run so they say, and that's the way things ought to be! If exercising is going to lead to a sports injury, or some long-term injury it's better not to exercise! This is one of the reasons why it is recommended to get the help of a physical trainer while working out.

- **Power Walking**

A little bit of brisk walking can help in weight loss. If you think your body is strong enough, try 20-30 minutes of power walking. A brisk power walk has overall health benefits and is useful for people who don't have any other activity planned and have just an hour or two after work.

- **Yoga**

Yoga is just great for the body because it makes you stretch. There are many parts of the body that receive little to no blood circulation, because of a sedentary lifestyle and the general lack of exercise. Gentle Yoga can help you there. There are lots of overweight women who benefit from doing a little yoga. Yoga has innumerable benefits for the body in terms of improving flexibility and aiding in weight-loss as well! It also helps to keep muscles supple.

- **Dance Classes**

Some people might overlook the obvious benefits of shaking a leg at a dance class like Salsa or Jive Class. However, these dance classes will get you out of breath with their quick moves and the necessity to adhere to the posture and form. Having a dance teacher to guide you will bring the best in you, improve your technique, while keeping you energetic. Attending dance classes and the practice you do at home, will lead to increased activity and make you lose more weight than ever before!

- **Jogging or "Wogging"**

is also a great exercise option. Mixing a combination of jogging and walking is also known as Wogging. Wogging is a great option for you if you think your body can handle it- you need to wear proper shoes, and you need to check your form. Doing this will prevent any muscle-related injury. There are many apps that help with training for your first 5K. These are the best for teaching you to jog or run because they involve a combination of walking and jogging. Some examples of these apps are Runmore and C25k

Any form of Slow Steady Paced Cardio can be helpful in weight-loss! It not only gets your heart pumping, it gets the body into fat burning mode. It also helps burn fat! Slow Steady Paced Cardio can include dancing, or slow to moderate aerobics. Again, stop when you are tired, and keep a bottle of water close by.

- **HIIT/Cardio/Zumba/Aerobics**

HIIT which is also called High-Intensity Interval Training is for the ones who are physically fit, and are looking to build endurance. There are a number of great HIIT workouts to be found on the internet, which help in burning fat and increasing the muscle to fat ratio. Youtube is your best source. Exercising with a trainer is also a good idea, sometimes a better idea because they remind you when to stop and not to push too hard or go too fast.

Like HIIT training workouts there are a number of other workouts one can do like Cardio, Zumba and Aerobics. The best part about these types of exercise sessions is that they are energetic, and they get your body temperature up, and calories burning while breaking a sweat! Ofcourse, this sort of energetic workout is not for everyone. Its always considered helpful to consult a doctor before starting any exercise program, if you are obese, above 35, or pregnant.

A few noteworthy advantages of Exercise

- helps with weight loss

- exercise lowers blood pressure

- it definitely improves cardiac health

- better believe it, exercise helps you to sleep better

- increases muscle mass

And so you thought Sleep Hygiene wasn't a thing!

Sleep is so very important for weight loss!

Maintaining a regular sleep schedule is one of the best things you can do for yourself.

Since sleep is the time our body regenerates, it's a really good idea to sleep at least 7-8 hrs every night.

As simple as it sounds, and something people tend to overlook, a shocking percentage of working adults get enough sleep in the modern world.

A good laugh and a long sleep are the two best cures for anything - Irish Proverb

Reasons to sleep more!

There really is a Good enough reason to sleep more! It can help you lose weight! Not only does a good night's rest do wonderful things like guarantee weight loss (because you'll be sleeping more and eating less!) A lot of other things are said to happen in our sleep like restoration and healing. Not only are people who sleep more less stressed out, research has actually shown that there is a connection between sleeping well and maintaining a healthy weight!

Apparently science has also proven that there is a reason why some people are obese! They don't sleep enough! Kids who don't sleep, often skip breakfast in the morning. Studies have also shown that kids who don't sleep crave sweeter or saltier snacks! As if they weren't having enough!

What is 'Sleep Quality'?

Sleep quality is the question of whether one's sleep is restful and restorative. It is also a useful indicator of whether a person is getting enough sleep. A person needs to sleep at least 7-8 hrs a night!

Benefits to improving ones 'Sleep Quality'?

Making a habit of eating at least 2 hrs before bed leads to better digestion

- Reduction in Stress

- Increased ability to deal with negative emotions

- People who sleep less tend to choose foods with higher calories

- Reduced risk of cardiovascular diseases, diabetes and other related diseases

- Get along better with others

And a lot more!

How much sleep do I need?

Good quality sleep is essential! Sleeping well equates to more than just feeling well-rested! Getting at least 8 hours of sleep a night is essential! During sleep a lot of restorative functions take place, and the body is said to heal itself naturally during sleep. You can't go wrong with eight hours of sleep a night! Most people do not get enough sleep out of choice or because of things like work, or a busy routine.

Anyways 8 hours of uninterrupted sleep is useful for the body and has a ton of benefits! Sleep is important for the body and people who get enough sleep are actually doing themselves a huge favor. Remember to get at least 7-8 hours of sleep a night as it aids in weight loss too.

Some tips for sleeping well include:

Taking a warm bath before you decide to go to sleep can be a really relaxing activity! Other ways to fall asleep include drinking some hot tea, reading a book and/or listening to calming music!

Alternatively, you can practice restorative yoga. It is known to relax a person and relieve stress from the last few hours of the day. Keep your phone in another room. Remember that you need to get at least 7-8 hrs of sleep every night! There's a reason why they call it beauty sleep !

After Weight Loss …Yahoo! Skinny You benefits!

So, you managed to lose 5 pounds! You have already reduced a dress size!

However, that's not the end of your weight loss journey!

Now that you've lost a couple of pounds, you realize there's room to improve!

You can set new goals and be a new person! You can learn to fall in love with your reflection!

"Make time for it. Just get it done. Nobody ever got strong or got in shape by thinking about it. They did it." –

Jim Wendler

You might have won the battle. But you didn't win the war!

There's nothing worse in life than doing what my friend Ryna did after she lost weight. After a month of healthy eating and making mindful food choices, she finally did manage to lose weight. That's the Good part. But the only mistake she made - she wore the same old clothes!

If you have noticed, most of the world's most brainy women, lose weight only so they can fit into a dress. But what Ryna did was so wrong! My book never mentions losing a dress size as the only motivation behind weight-loss efforts and exercise! Though it is one of the great perks of losing weight!

Buy new clothes!

If you ever lose weight, go shopping! Buy new jeans! Perhaps you were wearing only umbrella style dresses because you couldnt fit into anything else in the past. Now that you have lost the weight, try and Invest in a good pair of Skinny jeans and show off that toned waist. Stop wearing your old loose dresses you will probably float in them by now and will only make you look ugly.

You know how it is when you lose weight! It's only the fat folks that have issues in looking good in clothes! Skinny people look good in anything and everything. Buy clothes that look good on you! There might have been a nicer dress that you were eyeing on the rack, that was a size 12 but you wouldn't fit into it because you were a size 18!

Other than just buying tighter stuff, remember that when you lose weight you can wear stuff that is more risque. Wearing low-rise jeans for instance isn't a big thing for someone who has washboard abs. You might not have gotten that far, but that's just an example!

Experiment with new styles, cuts and colors! It's worth it to bust a little cash on an updated wardrobe! You will look totally different very unlike my friend Ryna who was floating in her old dresses!

Change your hairstyle!

Changing the way you do your hair could be a really great idea! Why not do it? (Save pictures of models that you see in the newspaper or in magazines. Take a screenshot of your phone when watching a random video) Put in the effort because sometimes a poor stylist would be as confused as you are. Put in the effort and take these pictures along with you, on your next salon visit. Try getting bangs at your next salon appointment, or layers if you never tried these styles before. Sometimes a complicated up-do that the stylist suggests may not be the best fit for you! Sometimes things go better when you do your own homework!

Do your make up differently!

Perhaps you have bought new clothes and changed your hairstyle. The next step is to experiment a little with new makeup styles. There are a variety of makeup techniques that stylists employ to tone down a face and to make it appear more toned. The use of a contour stick for example will highlight your cheekbones giving the face a sharper look.

Highlighting the eyes and lips is also a good idea. Do up your eyes with your favorite kajal and apply a bolder color like a light blue or light purple without the fear of looking like it looks too artificial or made up. Remember also that selfies tend to be easier to take, and angles easier to capture with a smaller more toned face.

Take some good 'before' and 'after' pics to post on Social Media!

This is a ritual almost among women when they lose weight. When you get a lot of compliments on your weight-loss progress pictures it is such a great feeling! Take pictures of you in your old size next to the new you in your new size (and wearing some fashionable clothes with your hair and makeup on fleek!) Post both the pictures side-by-side on social media!
The biggest fan of these pictures will of course be you! And imagine how great you will feel when you go through the innumerable compliments applauding your success!

Many salons do professional makeovers. You might have looked completely different before but try to make the most of the lifestyle change. Sometimes people have the habit of saying adverse things about other people that have put in the effort to lose weight. "You're looking so thin"

You can win in life and in the weight loss battle if you update your wardrobe and do your hair and make-up differently. Remember that the body positivity movement is not meant to encourage people to live unhealthy lifestyles.

It's meant to encourage people to love themselves for who they are.

More about the Body Positivity Movement

The Body Positivity Movement is a social movement based on the ideology that all female figures are created equal regardless of the shape they are in. It is a movement that was propounded by plus size international model Ashley Graham. The Body Positivity Movement celebrates all women no matter their weight.

You may have lost a little bit of weight, but that does not mean you stare at skinny models on social media. There is a long process before you ever actually acheive a size 6 or a size 8. For you the ideal dress size might be a size 12 or a size 16. Whatever be the case, celebrate the real you, just because of the Body Positivity Movement!